A COMPREHENSIVE GUIDE TO EXPLORING CALIFORNIA

Discover the Best Places to Visit, Activities, and Cuisine in The Golden State

Randy M. Greene

Table of Contents:

Introduction

California, also known as the Golden State, is located on the West Coast of the United States. With a population of over 39 million people, California is the most populous state in the country and is home to a diverse and thriving culture. From bustling cities like Los Angeles and San Francisco, to natural wonders like Yosemite National Park and Lake Tahoe, California has something for everyone.

Climate and Best Time to Visit

California's climate varies greatly depending on the region, but the state is generally known for its warm and dry summers and mild, wet winters. Coastal areas tend to have a Mediterranean climate, while the interior is typically more arid. The best time to visit California depends on your personal preferences and the activities you plan to participate in. Summer is the peak tourist season and is ideal for outdoor activities, such as surfing and hiking, while winter is a great time for skiing and snowboarding. If you prefer milder temperatures and fewer crowds, spring and fall are also good options.

Transportation Options

Getting around California is easy and convenient, with a variety of transportation options available. The state is served by several major airports, including Los Angeles International Airport (LAX) and San Francisco International Airport (SFO), as well as a comprehensive network of highways and public transportation systems, including buses and trains. Renting a car is a popular option for those who prefer to have the freedom and flexibility to explore the state on their own, while bicycle and walking tours are also available for those who prefer a more environmentally friendly mode of transportation.

California is a diverse and dynamic state that offers a wealth of opportunities for exploration and adventure. Whether you're interested in experiencing the vibrant culture of its cities, the natural beauty of its parks and beaches, or the rich history and heritage of its people, California is sure to leave you with unforgettable memories.

Attractions and Activities

California is a playground for outdoor enthusiasts, offering a diverse range of activities and attractions to suit every interest and skill level. Whether you want to go hiking, camping, or skiing in the mountains, or enjoy surfing, sunbathing, or whale watching at the beach, California has it all. In addition to its natural beauty, California is also home to several world-class theme parks, including Disneyland, Universal StudiosHollywood, and Six Flags Magic Mountain.

The state is also known for its rich cultural heritage, with numerous museums, art galleries, and historic landmarks to explore. The Getty Center in Los Angeles, the California Palace of the Legion of Honor in San Francisco, and the mission San Juan

Capistrano are just a few of the many cultural attractions that California has to offer.

Food and Drink

California is a foodie's paradise, with a thriving culinary scene that draws on a diverse range of influences and ingredients. From fresh seafood and Mexican cuisine to Chinese and Italian food, California has something for everyone. The state is also renowned for its wine, with several world-class wineries located in Napa and Sonoma valleys. Whether you prefer to dine at a fancy restaurant or enjoy a casual meal at a local diner,California has a range of dining options to suit your budget and taste.

Overview of California

California is a state located on the West Coast of the United States and is known for its diverse landscape, rich cultural heritage, and thriving economy. The state is the most populous in the country, with a population of over 39 million people, and is a hub of innovation and creativity. California is also renowned for its cuisine, wine industry, and beautiful beaches.

Geography and Climate

California covers an area of 163,696 square miles and is bordered by Oregon to the north, Nevada to the east, and Arizona to the southeast. The state is divided into several distinct regions, including the Coast Ranges, the Central Valley, the Sierra Nevada Mountains, and the Mojave Desert. The climate in California varies greatly, with the coastal areas having a Mediterranean climate and the interior being more arid. Summer Is typically warm and dry, while winter is mild and wet.

Economy and Major Industries

California is the world's fifth largest economy and is known for its thriving technology and entertainment industries. The state is home to numerous Fortune 500 companies, including Apple, Google, and Facebook, and is a hub of innovation and entrepreneurship. California isalso a major producer of agricultural products, including wine, almonds, and avocados, and is a major tourist destination, attracting millions of visitors each year.

Culture and Heritage

California is a melting pot of cultures, with a rich and diverse cultural heritage that is reflected in its food, art, and architecture. The state is home to several major cities,

including Los Angeles, San Francisco, and San Diego, which are known for their vibrant arts scenes, bustling nightlife, and rich cultural heritage. California is also home to several historic landmarks and museums, including the Getty Center in Los Angeles, the California Palace of the Legion of Honor in San Francisco, and the mission San Juan Capistrano, which offer a glimpse into the state's rich history and heritage.

California's options for transportation

Getting around California is easy and convenient, with a variety of transportation options available to meet the needs of visitors. Whether you prefer to travel by car, public transportation, or on foot, there are plenty of options to suit your budget and travel style.

Car Rentals

Renting a car is a popular option for those who prefer to have the freedom and flexibility to explore California on their own. The state is served by several major airports, including Los Angeles International Airport (LAX) and San Francisco International Airport (SFO), which offer car rental services. Renting a car is ideal for those who want to see the sights at their own pace and explore the state'smany scenic drives.

Public Transportation

California is served by a comprehensive network of public transportation systems, including buses and trains. The state's major cities, including Los Angeles, San Francisco, and San Diego, have extensive public transportation systems that are convenient and affordable. Public transportation is a great option for those who prefer totravel environmentally friendly, and it is also an excellent way to get around the city without having to worry about parking and traffic.

Walking and Biking Tours

Walking and biking tours are a great way to explore California's cities and scenic areas. The state is home to several bike-friendly cities, including San Francisco and Davis, which offer extensive bike lanes and bike rental services. Walking tours are also available in many cities, and are a great way to get an up-close and personal look at the local culture, architecture, and history.

Air Travel

California is served by several major airports, including Los Angeles International Airport (LAX), San Francisco International Airport (SFO), and San Diego International Airport (SAN). These airports offer direct flights to and from cities across the United States and around the world, making air travel a convenient and efficient way to get to California.

Ridesharing Services

Ridesharing services, such as Uber and Lyft, are widely available in California, and offer a convenient and affordable way to get around the state's major cities. Ridesharing services are ideal for those who want a more flexible and convenient transportation option, and are a great way to get to and from the airport or to explore the city without having to worry about parking and traffic.

Trains

California is served by several train services, including the Amtrak California, which offers daily services along the Pacific Coast and throughout the state. The Amtrak California is a convenient and affordable way to get around the state, and is an excellent option for those who want to enjoy the scenic views of California's countryside and coastline.

Ferries

California is home to several ferry services, including the San Francisco Bay Ferry, which offers daily services to several destinations in the Bay Area, including Alameda, Oakland, and Vallejo. Ferries are a convenient and scenic way to get around the Bay Area and are an excellent option for those who want to explore the region's many beaches, parks, and attractions.

In conclusion, California offers a wide range of transportation options, including car rentals, public transportation, walking and biking tours, air travel, ridesharing services, trains, and ferries. So whether you're looking to explore the state's bustling cities or its scenic countryside, California has a transportation option that's right for you.

Destinations in California You Must Visit

California is one of the most diverse and fascinating states in the United States, offering a wealth of must-see destinations for visitors. From bustling cities and picturesque towns to breathtaking natural landscapes and world-famous attractions, California has something to offer everyone. Here are some of the must-see destinations in California that you won't want to miss:

San Francisco:
San Francisco is one of the most iconic cities in California, renowned for its hilly terrain, Victorian architecture, and diverse neighborhoods. Must-see attractions in San

Francisco include the Golden Gate Bridge, Fisherman's Wharf, Alcatraz Island, and the cable cars, which offer breathtaking views of the city.

Los Angeles:
Los Angeles is the entertainment capital of the world and home to some of the most famous attractions in California, including Hollywood, Disneyland, Universal Studios, and the Santa Monica Pier. The city is also home to some of the most iconic beaches in California, including Venice Beach, Malibu, and Santa Monica Beach.

Napa Valley:
Napa Valley is one of the world's premier wine-growing regions and a must-see destination for wine lovers. Visitors can take wine tours, visit vineyards, and sample some of the finest wines in the world. The valley isalso home to several charming towns,

including Napa, Yountville, and St. Helena, which offer world-class dining, shopping, and accommodations.

Lake Tahoe:
Lake Tahoe is a stunning alpine lake surrounded by breathtaking mountains and forests. The lake is a popular destination for outdoor enthusiasts, offering opportunities for hiking, skiing, boating, fishing, and more. Visitors can also enjoy scenic drives around the lake, explore the many beaches and parks, and take in the stunning views of the surrounding mountains.

Yosemite National Park:
Yosemite National Park is one of the most iconic national parks in the United States and a must-see destination for nature lovers. The park is home to some of the most breathtaking landscapes in California, including El Capitan, Half Dome, and

Yosemite Falls, as well as a variety of wildlife, including black bears, deer, and coyotes.

Monterey Bay:
Monterey Bay is a picturesque coastal town that is famous for its stunning natural beauty and rich marine life. Visitors can take boat tours to see the area's famous sea otters, seals, and whales, or explore the nearby beaches and forests. The town is also home to several world-class aquariums, including the Monterey Bay Aquarium, which is a must-see attraction for families and nature lovers.

San Diego:
San Diego is a vibrant coastal city that is famous for its sunny weather, beautiful beaches, and world-class attractions. Must-see attractions in San Diego include Balboa Park, the San Diego Zoo, and La Jolla

Cove, as well as the USS Midway Museum, which is one of the largest and most impressive aircraft carriers in the world.

It's also important to note that California is home to some of the world's most famous festivals and events, including the Coachella Valley Music and Arts Festival, the Monterey Jazz Festival, and the San Francisco International Film Festival. If you're visiting California during one of these events, be sure to book your tickets and accommodations in advance, as they can sell out quickly.

In addition to these must-see destinations, California is also home to a variety of unique and unusual attractions that are worth checking out. For example, the Salton Sea is a vast, salty lake located in the desert that is home to a variety of strange and exotic creatures. The Madeline Flower Fields in Carlsbad is a colorful sea of vibrant blooms that covers 50 acres of rolling hills, and the Mystery Spot in Santa Cruz is a strange gravity-defying area that defies explanation.

Here are a few more must-see destinations in California that you may want to add to your itinerary:

☐ Santa Barbara: This charming coastal town is known for its Spanish-style architecture, beautiful beaches, and world-class wineries. Visitors can stroll the historic downtown area, sample local wines, and take in the stunning views of the Pacific Ocean.

☐ Big Sur: This breathtaking stretch of coastline along California's Central Coast is one of the most beautiful and dramatic in the world. Visitors can drive the famous Pacific Coast Highway, hike in the stunning redwood forests, and take in the breathtaking views of the rocky coastline.

☐ Joshua Tree National Park: This unique and otherworldly park is located in the California desert and is home to a variety of strange and unusual rock formations, as well as a wide variety of desert wildlife. Visitors can hike the park's many trails, climb the towering rock formations, or simply take in the stunning desert scenery.

☐ The Mission Trail: This historic trail winds through California's Central Coast and is home to a series of historic Spanish missions that were established in the late 1700s. Visitors can explore the missions, learn about the history of California's Spanish colonial period, and take in the beautiful coastal scenery.

☐ Hearst Castle: This stunning estate was built by media mogul William Randolph Hearst and is located on the Central Coast of California. Visitors can tour the castle's many rooms and gardens, learn about Hearst's life and career, and take in the breathtaking views of the surrounding coastline.

☐ Lake Tahoe: This stunning alpine lake is located in the Sierra Nevada mountain range and is known for its crystal-clear waters, stunning scenery, and outdoor recreation opportunities. Visitors can swim, boat, hike, ski, and take in the breathtaking views of the surrounding mountains.

☐ Monterey Bay Aquarium: This world-renowned aquarium is located on the Central Coast of California and is home to a vast collection of marine life, including sea otters, jellyfish, and sea horses. Visitors can watch live demonstrations, touch tanks, and explore the many exhibits to learn about the ocean and its inhabitants.

- ☐ The California Redwoods: These massive trees are found along California's northern coast and are some of the tallest and oldest living organisms on earth. Visitors can hike through the redwood forests, marvel at the towering trees, and take in the beauty of the surrounding landscape.
- ☐ The Wine Country: California is home to some of the world's best wineries and vineyards, and visitors can explore this famous wine-making region and sample local wines, tour wineries, and take in the stunning scenery.
- ☐ The Getty Center: This stunning museum is located in Los Angeles and is home to an impressive collection of art, architecture, and manuscripts.

Visitors can tour the galleries, enjoy the beautiful gardens and architecture, and take in the breathtaking views of the city.

The Golden Gate Bridge is one of the most iconic landmarks in California and is a must-visit destination for anyone traveling to the San Francisco Bay Area. Here are a few more details about this famous bridge:

- History: The Golden Gate Bridge was built in the 1930s and is named for the Golden Gate Strait, which is the entrance to the San Francisco Bay from the Pacific Ocean. The bridge was designed by chief engineer Joseph Strauss and was a massive engineering feat at the time, taking nearly four years to complete.

- Design: The Golden Gate Bridge is a suspension bridge, meaning that it is supported by cables that are anchored to two massive concrete towers on either side of the strait. The bridge spans 1.7 miles and is one of the longest suspension bridges in the world.

- Views: One of the most popular things to do on the Golden Gate Bridge is to walk or bike across it and take in the stunning views of the San Francisco Bay and the Pacific Ocean. On a clear day, you can see all the way to the Farallon Islands, which are located more than 30 miles off the coast.

- Landmarks: The Golden Gate Bridge is located near several other famous landmarks in San Francisco, including Alcatraz Island, Fisherman's Wharf, and the Presidio. Visitors can easily combine a visit to the bridge with a tour of these other famous destinations.

- Facts: Some fun facts about the Golden Gate Bridge include that it was painted International Orange to increase visibility in the fog, the total weight of the bridge is more than 887,000 tons, and it is painted every year to keep it looking its best.

These are just a few more details about the Golden Gate Bridge, one of California's most iconic landmarks. Whether you're a history buff, an architecture aficionado, or just looking for a great place to take in the views, you won't want to miss this famous bridge.

La Jolla Cove is a picturesque beach located in La Jolla, California, just north of San

Diego. Here are a few more details about this stunning destination:

- ☐ Location: La Jolla Cove is located in the heart of La Jolla and is easily accessible from many of the surrounding hotels, shops, and restaurants. The cove is surrounded by cliffs, which provide a stunning backdrop for the turquoise waters of the Pacific Ocean.

- ☐ Wildlife: La Jolla Cove is a popular spot for watching wildlife, including seals, sea lions, and various species of birds. Visitors can often spot these animals sunbathing on the rocks near the cove, and during certain times of year, they may even be able to swim with sea lions in the nearby waters.

☐ Activities: There are plenty of activities to enjoy at La Jolla Cove, including swimming, sunbathing, snorkeling, and kayaking. Visitors can rent equipment on the beach or sign up for guided tours to get an up-close look at the local wildlife and the underwater world.

☐ Scenery: The scenery at La Jolla Cove is simply breathtaking, with crystal-clear waters, white sand beaches, and towering cliffs. Visitors can take a leisurely stroll along the beach, relax on the sand, or simply sit and soak up the sun while taking in the stunning views.

☐ Surrounding Area: La Jolla Cove is located in the heart of La Jolla, which is known for its upscale shopping, dining, and entertainment. Visitors can explore the many shops, galleries, and restaurants in the area, or take a stroll through the nearby parks and gardens.

In addition to these attractions, there are several other reasons to visit La Jolla Cove:

☐ Accessibility: La Jolla Cove is easily accessible, with ample parking available nearby and a number of public transportation options, making it a great destination for visitors of all ages and abilities.

☐ Safety: La Jolla Cove is a well-patrolled beach, with lifeguards on duty during the summer months to ensure the safety of visitors. There are also designated swim and surf zones, making it a great place for families with young children.

☐ Cleanliness: La Jolla Cove is known for its clean and well-maintained beaches, making it a great destination for those who appreciate natural beauty and a sense of serenity.

☐ Amenities: There are plenty of amenities available at La Jolla Cove, including restrooms, showers, and picnic areas, making it a great destination for a day trip or a weekend getaway.

☐ Events: La Jolla Cove is also the site of several annual events, including beach volleyball tournaments, music concerts, and art fairs, making it a great destination for visitors who want to experience the local culture.

These are just a few more reasons to visit La Jolla Cove, one of California's most picturesque and accessible beaches. Whether you're a local resident or a visiting tourist, you won't want to miss this stunning destination.

Activities and Experiences in California:

California is home to a wide variety of activities and experiences, making it a great destination for visitors of all ages and interests. Here are a few of the many options available:

- Outdoor Activities: With its diverse landscapes, California is a paradise for outdoor enthusiasts. Visitors can go hiking in the many state and national parks, take a scenic drive along the Pacific Coast Highway, or go mountain biking in the Santa Cruz Mountains. There are also many opportunities for water activities, such as surfing, kayaking, and stand-up paddleboarding.

- Arts and Culture: California is a hub for the arts, with world-renowned museums, galleries, and theaters. Visitors can explore the many art museums in Los Angeles, including the Getty Center, or attend a performance at the San Francisco Opera or the Los Angeles Philharmonic. There are also many street art installations and murals to discover in cities like San Francisco and Los Angeles.
- Food and Wine: California is known for its farm-to-table cuisine, with many restaurants showcasing local and seasonal ingredients. Visitors can go

wine tasting in Napa and Sonoma, or sample the fresh seafood in San Francisco and Monterey. There are also many food festivals and events throughout the state, such as the Golden State Tattoo & Music Festival in Sacramento and the California Avocado Festival in Carpinteria.

- Theme Parks: California is home to some of the world's most popular theme parks, including Disneyland in Anaheim and Universal Studios Hollywood. Visitors can enjoy thrilling rides and attractions, as well as meet their favorite characters and enjoy live shows and parades.

- Sports: California is a sports lover's paradise, with many professional teams, including the Los Angeles Lakers, the San Francisco Giants, and the San Francisco 49ers. Visitors can also attend a game at one of the many college stadiums, such as the Memorial Stadium in Berkeley or the Rose Bowl in Pasadena.

- Hiking: California is home to many beautiful state and national parks, offering a wide range of hiking trails for visitors of all skill levels. Some popular hiking destinations include Yosemite National Park, with its iconic waterfalls and granite cliffs, and Redwood National and State Parks, home to some of the tallest trees in the world.

- Surfing: California is known for its great waves, making it a popular destination for surfers. Visitors can take lessons or rent equipment at many of the state's beaches, including Newport Beach, Huntington Beach, and Santa Cruz.

- Mountain Biking: California is a great destination for mountain bikers, with many trails and parks offering a wide range of riding experiences. Some popular destinations include the Downieville Downhill in the Sierra Nevada mountains and the Mount Tamalpais State Park near San Francisco.

- Rock Climbing: California is also a popular destination for rock climbers, with many climbing routes and parks offering challenging climbs for both beginners and experienced climbers. Some popular destinations include Joshua Tree National Park, with its unique rock formations, and Pinnacles National Park, known for its spires and pinnacles.
- Water Sports: California is also home to many lakes and rivers, making it a great destination for water sports enthusiasts. Visitors can go kayaking, stand-up paddleboarding, or rafting in

many of the state's waterways, including Lake Tahoe, the American River, and the Merced River.

In addition to outdoor adventures, California offers many other activities and experiences that visitors can enjoy. Here are a few more details:

1. Food and Wine: California is famous for its food and wine, making it a great destination for foodies and wine lovers. Visitors can sample the state's famous cuisine, including fresh seafood, farm-to-table dishes, and world-class wines, at many of the state's top restaurants and wineries. Some popular food and wine destinations include Napa Valley, known for its premium wines and gourmet cuisine, and San Francisco, known for its diverse and innovative food scene.

California is known for its diverse and innovative food scene, and visitors can experience some of the best cuisine in the world in cities like San Francisco and Los Angeles. In addition to traditional American fare, California offers a range of culinary experiences, including:

Farm-to-Table Restaurants: California is home to many farm-to-table restaurants, where chefs use locally sourced ingredients to create delicious and healthy dishes. These restaurants are a great way to taste the local flavors of California and enjoy fresh, seasonal ingredients.

- Ethnic Cuisine: With a large and diverse population, California offers a wide variety of ethnic cuisine, including Mexican, Asian, Indian, and Italian, just to name a few. Visitors can find authentic, flavorful dishes in cities like San Francisco, Los Angeles, and San Diego.

- Street Food: California is famous for its street food scene, with food trucks and stalls offering everything from tacos to Thai food. Visitors can enjoy quick and delicious bites on the go, or gather with friends for a street food festival.

- Craft Breweries and Wineries: California is a leader in the craft brewery and wine industries, and visitors can sample some of the state's best beers and wines at taprooms and tasting rooms throughout the region. Some popular destinations include Napa Valley, Sonoma County, and the Santa Barbara wine country.

- Cocktails: California is home to many talented mixologists who create unique and creative cocktails using local ingredients and innovative techniques. Visitors can enjoy classic drinks and signature creations at bars and lounges in cities like San Francisco, Los Angeles, and San Diego.

2. Art and Culture: California is also home to many world-class museums, galleries, and theaters, making it a great destination for those who appreciate art and culture. Visitors can explore the collections of the Getty Center in Los Angeles, the Museum of Modern Art in San Francisco, and the Museum of the American West in San Francisco.

California has many other cultural attractions that are worth exploring. Some highlights include:

- Golden Gate Park: Golden Gate Park is a large urban park in San Francisco that is home to many cultural institutions, including the de Young Museum, the Japanese Tea Garden, and the California Academy of Sciences. Visitors can explore the park's many gardens, lakes, and walking trails, as well as its cultural attractions.

- Hollywood Walk of Fame: The Hollywood Walk of Fame is a famous sidewalk in Hollywood, Los Angeles, that is lined with the stars of some of the biggest names in entertainment. Visitors can take a walk down the sidewalk and see the stars of their favorite actors, musicians, and other celebrities.

- Fisherman's Wharf: Fisherman's Wharf is a popular neighborhood in San

Francisco that is famous for its seafood restaurants, street performers, and historic ships. Visitors can enjoy fresh seafood, watch street performers, and explore the historic ships that are moored at the wharf.

- Getty Center: The Getty Center is a museum in Los Angeles that is dedicated to the arts and humanities. Visitors can explore the museum's collections, which include works of art, manuscripts, and photographs, as well as its beautiful gardens and outdoor spaces.

- Mission San Juan Capistrano: Mission San Juan Capistrano is a historic Spanish mission in Orange County, California, that was founded in 1776. Visitors can explore the mission's museum, gardens, and other buildings, and learn about the history of California's Spanish mission system.

3. Sports: California is also a great destination for sports fans, with many professional sports teams, including the Los Angeles Lakers, the San Francisco Giants, and the Los Angeles Dodgers. Visitors can attend live games and cheer on their favorite teams in some of the best sports venues in the world.

4. Wine Tasting: California is famous for its wine industry, and visitors can sample some of the state's best wines at wineries and tasting rooms throughout the region. Some popular wine-tasting destinations include Napa Valley, Sonoma County, and the Santa Barbara wine country.

5. Theme Parks: California is home to some of the world's best theme parks,

including Disneyland, Universal Studios Hollywood, and Six Flags Magic Mountain. Visitors can enjoy thrilling rides, shows, and attractions at these parks, making them a great choice for families and adrenaline seekers.

6. Beaches: With over 1,000 miles of coastline, California has some of the most beautiful beaches in the world. Visitors can relax on the sand, surf, swim, or just enjoy the scenery at popular beaches like Venice Beach, Newport Beach, and La Jolla Cove.

7. Culinary Experiences: California is known for its diverse and innovative food scene, and visitors can experience some of the best cuisine in the world in cities like San Francisco and Los Angeles. From farm-to-table restaurants to street food stalls, there's something for everyone in California

Accommodation Option:

California offers a range of accommodation options to suit every budget and travel style. Popular choices comprise:

1. Hotels: California has a wide variety of hotels, ranging from budget-friendly options to luxury properties. Visitors can find hotels in all major cities and tourist destinations, as well as in more remote areas.

- Boutique hotels: Boutique hotels offer a unique and personalized experience for travelers. They often have smaller guest rooms and a more intimate atmosphere than traditional hotels. Boutique hotels are a great option for travelers who are looking for a stylish and chic place to stay.

- Luxury hotels: Luxury hotels offer a high level of comfort, service, and amenities for travelers. They often have spacious guest rooms, multiple dining options, and on-site spas and fitness centers. Luxury hotels are a great option for travelers who are looking for a pampering and indulgent experience.

2. Vacation rentals: Vacation rentals are a great option for travelers who are looking for a more home-like experience. They can range from apartments and condos to entire houses, and often come equipped with a kitchen and other amenities. Vacation rentals are a great option for families and groups of travelers who are looking for a more private and comfortable stay.

3. Bed and Breakfasts: Bed and breakfasts are a great option for visitors looking for a more personal and intimate travel experience. These properties often offer unique and historic accommodations and a more relaxed atmosphere.

4. Camping grounds: Camping grounds offer a unique way to experience the great outdoors in California. They offer tent and RV sites, as well as cabins and yurts for those who prefer a more comfortable experience. Camping grounds are a great option for nature lovers, families, and travelers who are looking for a budget-friendly option.

5. Hostels: Hostels are a budget-friendly option for travelers looking to save money on accommodation. Typically, they provide shared rooms, communal areas, and a lively atmosphere

When choosing an accommodation option in California, it's important to consider the location and proximity to attractions, as well as the facilities and amenities offered. For example, if you're planning on visiting theme parks, it may be convenient to stay in a hotel close to the park. If you're looking for a more relaxed and intimate experience, a bed and breakfast or vacation rental may be a better option.

Additionally, it's important to consider the time of year you'll be visiting California. During peak tourist season, prices for hotels and other accommodations may be higher, so it's important to book in advance to ensure availability and the best prices.

To make the most of your trip to California, it's also important to consider your budget and what's important to you in terms of amenities and services. Whether you're looking for a luxurious spa experience or a more basic, budget-friendly option, California has a range of accommodation options to suit every need and budget.

When booking your accommodation in California, it's also important to consider the type of trip you're planning. For example, if you're planning a road trip, it may be convenient to book a vacation rental or camping ground that allows you to park your car nearby. If you're planning to travel with children, it may be important to choose a hotel or vacation rental with family-friendly amenities, such as a pool or playground.

Another factor to consider is the type of activities and experiences you're interested in. For example, if you're interested in beach activities, it may be convenient to choose a hotel or vacation rental located near the beach. If you're interested in exploring the local culture and arts, it may be convenient to choose a hotel or vacation rental located near cultural attractions.

Here are some additional tips to help you make the most of your accommodation options in California:

- ☐ Consider location: When choosing your accommodation, consider the location. Are you looking for a quiet and peaceful location, or do you want to be in the heart of the action? Do you want to be near the beach, or do you prefer the mountains? The location of your accommodation can greatly impact your experience, so take the time to find the perfect location for your needs.

☐ Book early: Popular tourist destinations in California can fill up quickly, especially during peak travel seasons. Booking your accommodation early can help ensure that you have a place to stay and can also save you money.

☐ Consider off-peak seasons: Prices for accommodation can be significantly lower during off-peak seasons. Consider traveling during the shoulder season, when the weather is still good but the crowds are smaller.

☐ Book in advance: Booking your accommodation in advance can help you secure a better rate and avoid price increases closer to your travel dates.

☐ Be flexible: Being flexible with your travel dates, location, and type of accommodation can help you find better rates and deals.

☐ Look for bundled packages: Some accommodations may offer bundled packages that include transportation, activities, and meals. These packages can often provide a better overall value than booking each item separately.

☐ Compare prices: Take the time to compare prices for different types of accommodations and locations to find the best value for your budget.

☐ Use loyalty programs: If you're a member of a hotel loyalty program, consider using your points or miles to book your accommodation.

☐ Take advantage of discounts: Many accommodations offer discounts for military personnel, senior citizens, and students. Make sure to ask about any discounts that may be available to you.

Going Off the Beaten Track: California

California is known for its world-famous tourist destinations, but there's much more to this state beyond the typical tourist trail. Here are some unique experiences that allow you to explore California beyond the usual hotspots:

1. Visit the Channel Islands: Located off the coast of California, the Channel Islands are a group of five islands that offer stunning scenery, abundant wildlife, and a peaceful escape from the hustle and bustle of the mainland. Take a ferry from Ventura or Santa Barbara to visit these islands and enjoy activities such as kayaking, hiking, and snorkeling.

2. Explore the California Central Valley: The Central Valley is a vast agricultural region that runs through the heart of California. Here, you'll find rolling hills, fertile farmland, and charming small towns that are off the beaten path. Take a drive along the backroads, stop at local wineries, and visit historic landmarks such as the San Joaquin Mission in Stockton.

3. Discover the Eastern Sierra: The Eastern Sierra is a rugged and remote mountain range that is located in the eastern part of California. This area is home to breathtaking landscapes, including high alpine lakes, towering peaks, and pristine wilderness. Take a scenic drive along the Eastern Sierra Scenic Byway, and be sure to stop at Mono Lake, a unique and otherworldly body of water.

4. Visit the Redwood National and State Parks: The Redwood National and State Parks are located in northern California and are home to some of the tallest trees in the world. These parks offer incredible hiking and scenic drives, as well as opportunities to see a variety of wildlife, such as elk, bald eagles, and sea lions.
5. Experience the Gold Rush towns: The Gold Rush of 1849 brought thousands of people to California in search of riches. Today, many of the towns that were established during this time have been preserved and are open to visitors. Explore the well-preserved architecture, museums, and historic sites in these charming towns, such as Auburn, Placerville, and Coloma.
6. Visit the California Missions: California has a rich history that is closely tied to its Spanish colonial past.

The California Missions are a string of 21 missions that were built along the California coast by Spanish friars in the late 18th and early 19th centuries. These missions served as religious and cultural centers, and many of them have been preserved and are open to visitors.

7. Enjoy the California Deserts: The deserts of California are often overlooked by visitors, but they offer a unique and otherworldly landscape that is well worth exploring. Visit Joshua Tree National Park to see its iconic Joshua trees, rock formations, and diverse desert wildlife. The Anza-Borrego Desert State Park is another beautiful and diverse desert landscape, offering a range of outdoor activities, from hiking and camping to stargazing and wildflower viewing.

8. Discover the California Wine Country: California is famous for its wine, and the state's wine country is a must-visit for any wine lover. Napa Valley and Sonoma County are the most well-known wine regions, but there are many other, less crowded areas to explore, such as the Livermore Valley, the Santa Cruz Mountains, and the Sierra Foothills. Visit local wineries, sample the wines, and enjoy the scenic views of rolling hills and vineyards.

9. Explore California's State Parks: California has an extensive network of state parks that offer a wide range of outdoor experiences. From rugged coastal bluffs and redwood forests to desert landscapes and mountain peaks, these parks offer something for everyone. Whether you want to hike, bike, camp, or simply enjoy the

scenery, there's a state park in California that is perfect for you.

10. Visit the California Museums: California is home to a wealth of museums, many of which are world-renowned. From the Getty Center in Los Angeles to the de Young Museum in San Francisco, there are museums that offer a range of experiences, from art and culture to science and technology. Whether you're a history buff, an art lover, or simply enjoy learning something new, there's a museum in California that is perfect for you.

11. Visit California's Beaches: Beyond the famous surf spots and crowded beaches, there are many hidden gems to be found along California's coastline. Take a scenic drive along the Pacific Coast Highway to discover small coves and hidden beaches, or explore the

rugged coastline of Big Sur. Stop at beaches like Carmel-by-the-Sea, Half Moon Bay, or La Jolla Cove to enjoy breathtaking views and peaceful surroundings.

12. Explore California's Historic Gold Rush Country: In the mid-19th century, California was at the center of a gold rush that drew thousands of people from around the world in search of wealth and adventure. Today, visitors can explore the historic gold rush towns, pan for gold, and learn about this fascinating chapter in California's history.

13. Visit California's National Parks: California is home to some of the most stunning national parks in the United States, including Yosemite, Kings Canyon, and Sequoia National Parks. These parks offer breathtaking natural beauty, incredible hiking and camping

opportunities, and a chance to get up close and personal with California's unique wildlife.

14. Discover California's Agricultural Heartland: California is one of the largest agricultural producers in the world, and the state's Central Valley is the heart of this industry. Visitors can tour local farms, sample fresh produce, and learn about the state's rich agricultural heritage. From the vineyards of Napa Valley to the citrus orchards of the San Joaquin Valley, there's something for everyone in California's agricultural heartland.

15. Attend a Farmers Market: California is known for its fresh and delicious produce, and attending a local farmers market is a great way to experience the state's vibrant food culture. From the Ferry Building Farmers Market in San Francisco to the Hollywood Farmers

Market in Los Angeles, there's a farmers market for every taste and budget. You can sample local specialties, try new foods, and meet the farmers who grow the food you're eating.

16. Experience a Festival or Fair: California is home to many colorful and unique festivals and fairs that celebrate the state's diverse cultures and traditions. From the Sonoma County Fair to the San Diego County Fair, there's a festival or fair for every interest and season. You can enjoy live music, try delicious food, watch exciting competitions, and meet new people while you experience a unique aspect of California's vibrant culture.

17. Visit a Small Town: California is home to many charming small towns that offer a unique and authentic experience. Take a drive through the

rolling hills of wine country, or explore the historic streets of small towns like Ferndale or Nevada City. Small towns offer a unique look into California's history and culture, and often have a slower pace of life that's perfect for relaxing and rejuvenating.

18. Try a New Adventure Sport: California is known for its year-round mild climate, which makes it the perfect place to try new adventure sports. From surfing and kayaking to rock climbing and hiking, there's something for everyone in California. Take a lesson from a local expert, or simply grab your gear and hit the water or the trails for a unique and exciting experience.

19. Take a Sunset Cruise: California is known for its beautiful sunsets, and taking a sunset cruise is a great way to experience them. Whether you're in

San Francisco Bay, Los Angeles Harbor, or along the coast, you can enjoy the stunning scenery while you relax and unwind. Most sunset cruises offer drinks, snacks, and music, making them the perfect way to end a day of exploring California.

20. Take a Road Trip: Finally, one of the best ways to experience California is to simply get in your car and hit the road. Whether you're traveling up the Pacific Coast Highway, exploring the deserts of Joshua Tree, or cruising through wine country, a road trip is the perfect way to see and experience the state at your own pace. Stop at scenic viewpoints, try local foods, and make memories that will last a lifetime.

Getting Around in California:

California is a large and diverse state, and there are many ways to get around, whether you're exploring the bustling cities or the scenic countryside. This section will provide a comprehensive overview of the transportation options available to visitors and help you determine the best way to get around while you're in California.

☐ Public Transportation:
California has a comprehensive public transportation system, including buses, trains, and light rail. The state's largest cities, including Los Angeles, San Francisco, and San Diego, have extensive public transportation systems that provide convenient and affordable

access to many of the state's most popular attractions.

☐ Buses: California's public bus systems are extensive and offer a cost-effective way to get around. Most cities have local bus systems that connect with regional and inter-city bus services, providing access to many of the state's most popular destinations.

☐ Trains: California's trains are operated by Amtrak and provide service to many of the state's major cities, including Los Angeles, San Francisco, and San Diego. Amtrak also offers scenic routes through some of California's most beautiful landscapes, including the Pacific coastline and the wine country.

☐ Light Rail: Many cities in California, including San Francisco and San Diego, have light rail systems that provide a convenient and affordable alternative to buses and taxis. Light rail systems typically run on tracks and make limited stops, making them a quick and efficient way to get around.

☐ Rideshare Services: Rideshare services, such as Uber and Lyft, are widely available in California and provide a convenient and affordable way to get around, especially in cities where public transportation is limited. These services allow you to use your smartphone to book a ride, track the location of your driver, and pay for your ride.

☐ Taxi Services: Taxi services are also widely available in California and provide a convenient and affordable way to get around, especially in cities where public transportation is limited. Taxis can be hailed on the street or booked in advance, and they offer a flexible and convenient way to get around.

☐ Driving: Driving is a popular way to get around in California, especially for those visiting the state's rural and scenic areas. California's highways and roads are well-maintained and provide easy access to many of the state's popular attractions. However, traffic can be heavy in cities, especially during peak hours, so be prepared for slow-moving or congested roads.

☐ Biking: Biking is a popular way to get around in California, especially in cities like San Francisco and San Diego, which have extensive bike lane networks. Biking is a great way to get exercise and see the sights, but be aware that traffic can be heavy in cities, so be prepared for busy roads.

Additionally, visitors to California should be aware of some important tips when it comes to transportation:

- Plan ahead: If you're driving or taking public transportation, it's a good idea to plan your route in advance to avoid getting lost or stuck in traffic. You can use online maps or navigation apps to help plan your trip.
- Budget for transportation costs: Transportation can add up quickly in California, especially if you're using rideshare services, taxis, or rental cars. Make sure to budget for these costs in advance so you're not caught off guard.
- Be prepared for traffic: Traffic can be heavy in California, especially in cities like Los Angeles, San Francisco, and San Diego. Allow extra time for your travels and be prepared for delays.
- Know the rules of the road: California has specific rules and regulations when it comes to driving and using public transportation. Make sure to familiarize

yourself with these rules so you stay safe and avoid any fines or penalties.

- Take advantage of discounts: Many public transportation systems in California offer discounts for students, seniors, and those with disabilities. You may also be able to find discounts for museums, attractions, and other activities through your hotel or tour company.
- Rent a car or use public transportation: Renting a car is a convenient option for exploring California, especially if you're traveling with a group. However, it's also possible to get around using public transportation, such as buses, trains, and light rail. Consider both options and choose the one that works best for your travel style and budget.
- Use public transportation to save money: Public transportation is a cost-effective way to get around

California, especially if you're traveling to major cities like Los Angeles and San Francisco. You can often purchase passes that provide unlimited rides for a set period of time, which can save you money in the long run.

- Walk or bike in smaller towns: If you're visiting smaller towns in California, it's possible to get around on foot or by bike. This is a great way to see the sights and get some exercise at the same time. Make sure to bring comfortable walking shoes and appropriate clothing for the weather.

- Use ride-sharing apps: Ride-sharing apps like Uber and Lyft are available in many parts of California and can be a convenient option for getting around. Keep in mind that prices can vary based on demand and the time of day, so be prepared for fluctuating costs.

- Consider a guided tour: If you're new to California or if you want to learn more about the state's history and culture, consider taking a guided tour. Guided tours can provide you with an expert guide who will take you to all of the best places to visit, and give you a deeper understanding of the state and its people.
- Plan your route in advance: Before you head out, take some time to plan your route. This will help you avoid getting lost and will also ensure that you arrive at your destination on time. Use a map or navigation app to help you find your way.
- Check for traffic and road closures: Large cities in California, such as Los Angeles and San Francisco, can have heavy traffic at certain times of the day. Check for traffic and road closures

before you set out to ensure a smooth and stress-free drive.

- Park wisely: If you're driving and need to park your car, be sure to park in a safe and well-lit area. Avoid parking in isolated areas, and never leave valuables visible in your car.
- Know the laws: Make sure to familiarize yourself with the driving laws in California, including speed limits, seatbelt requirements, and laws related to cell phone use while driving.
- Take advantage of ride-sharing services: Another alternative to driving is using ride-sharing services like Uber or Lyft. These services are widely available in California and can be a convenient way to get around, especially in larger cities.
- Rent a bike: If you want to explore California at your own pace, consider renting a bike. There are many bike

rental shops throughout the state, and you can use a bike to explore scenic routes, beaches, and parks.

- Hire a car service: If you want to travel in comfort and style, consider hiring a car service. Many car services are available in California and can be a great option for airport transfers, city tours, and longer road trips.
- Use the airport shuttle: If you're arriving in California by plane, consider using the airport shuttle. Many airports in California offer shuttle services to popular tourist destinations, making it easy to get around without having to rent a car.

Aspects of Health and Safety

Safety and health considerations are important factors to consider when traveling to any destination, including California. Here are some tips to help you stay safe and healthy during your trip:

1. Get the appropriate vaccinations: Before you travel, check to see if any vaccinations are recommended or required for your trip. This information can usually be obtained from your doctor or a travel clinic.

2. Drink plenty of water: California can be hot and dry, especially in the summer months, so it's important to stay hydrated. Avoid alcohol and coffee since they can dehydrate you and make sure to drink enough of water.

3. Protect yourself from the sun: California is known for its sunny weather, but it's important to protect yourself from the sun's harmful rays. Wear protective clothing, use sunscreen, and take breaks in the shade when needed.

4. Take precautions against foodborne illness: To avoid foodborne illness, make sure to only eat food that has been cooked thoroughly and to drink bottled water instead of tap water.

5. Be cautious when participating in outdoor activities: If you plan on participating in outdoor activities, such as hiking or surfing, make sure to follow safety guidelines and be cautious of potential hazards, such as wildlife and strong currents.

6. Stay alert in crowded areas: California is a popular tourist destination, and it's important to stay alert in crowded

areas, such as tourist attractions and public transportation. Keep your valuables close and be aware of your surroundings.

7. Know the emergency services number: Familiarize yourself with the emergency services number for the area you're visiting, which is usually 911. Keep this number in your phone or written down in a safe place.

8. Purchase travel insurance: Travel insurance can provide coverage for unexpected medical expenses, trip cancellations, and other incidents that can occur during your trip. Consider purchasing travel insurance to provide peace of mind and financial protection.

9. Research local laws and customs: Before you travel, familiarize yourself with the local laws and customs in the area you're visiting. This can help you avoid unintentional cultural faux pas

and can also help keep you out of legal trouble.

10.   Avoid risky behavior: It's important to avoid risky behavior, such as excessive alcohol consumption, illegal drug use, and walking alone at night in unfamiliar areas. This can help you reduce your risk of injury and stay safe during your trip.

11.   Keep important documents with you: Keep important documents, such as your passport, travel itinerary, and emergency contact information, with you at all times. You may also want to make copies of these documents and leave them with a trusted friend or family member.

12.   Stay hydrated: California can be hot and dry, especially during the summer months, so it's important to stay hydrated. Make sure to drink plenty of water throughout the day, and consider

holding a water bottle that can be filled up.

13. Protect yourself from the sun: The sun in California can be intense, so make sure to protect yourself from the sun's harmful rays. Wear a hat, sunglasses, and use a high-SPF sunscreen to avoid sunburn and skin damage.

14. Be prepared for natural disasters: California is prone to natural disasters such as earthquakes, wildfires, and droughts. Make sure you know what to do in the event of an emergency and always stay informed of the latest weather conditions and alerts.

15. Practice food safety: When eating out in California, make sure to follow good food safety practices, such as avoiding undercooked food and raw vegetables, and only drinking bottled water.

16. Avoid wild animals: While California is home to a variety of wildlife, it's important to avoid wild animals, such as coyotes, mountain lions, and rattlesnakes. If you encounter a wild animal, it's best to back away slowly and avoid making sudden movements.

17. Avoid dangerous areas: Research the areas you plan to visit and be aware of any areas that are known to be unsafe or have high crime rates. Avoid these areas, especially at night.

18. Keep a low profile: Avoid drawing attention to yourself by wearing flashy or expensive jewelry and avoid carrying large amounts of cash.

19. Stay connected: Keep in touch with family and friends by sharing your travel itinerary and keeping them updated on your whereabouts. Consider using a international phone plan or

purchasing a local sim card to stay connected.

20. Take precautions against insect bites: California is home to various insects that can carry diseases. Use insect repellent, wear protective clothing, and take other measures to reduce your risk of being bitten.

21. Be aware of natural hazards: California is prone to earthquakes, fires, and other natural disasters. Stay informed about the latest weather and disaster warnings, and be prepared to evacuate if necessary.

22. Exercise caution when swimming: Many of California's beaches and lakes can have strong currents and other hazards, so it's important to always swim with a buddy and to only swim in areas designated for swimming.

23. Pack a first-aid kit: A small first-aid kit, including pain relievers, antiseptic

wipes, and any necessary prescription medications, is essential.

It's also a good idea to carry basic first-aid supplies, such as band-aids, pain relievers, and any necessary medications. Additionally, consider obtaining travel insurance that covers emergency medical expenses and evacuation in case of injury or illness.

When it comes to personal safety, always be aware of your surroundings, especially in unfamiliar areas. Keep valuables and important documents secure and consider using a money belt or other secure storage solution. If you're out late at night, stay in well-lit areas and avoid walking alone.

It's also important to be respectful of local laws and customs while in California. Familiarize yourself with the laws, including any restrictions on activities such as smoking or drinking in public, and respect the rights and privacy of others.

By following these tips, you can stay safe and secure while exploring all that California has to offer.

Culture and Customs of California

California is a melting pot of cultures, with a diverse population that includes people from all over the world. This diversity is reflected in the state's rich cultural heritage, which can be experienced through its art, music, food, and festivals.

☐ Art: California is home to a thriving art scene, with world-renowned museums and galleries showcasing works by local and international artists. The Getty Center in Los Angeles and the Museum of Modern Art in San Francisco are just two examples of the many cultural institutions that can be found in the state.

☐ Music: California is known for its music scene, which encompasses everything from classical orchestras to punk rock. The state is home to some of the most famous music venues in the world, including the Hollywood Bowl, the Fillmore in San Francisco, and the Greek Theatre in Los Angeles.

☐ Food: California's diverse population has led to a thriving food scene, with cuisine from all over the world available. From the fresh seafood in San Francisco to the Mexican street tacos in Los Angeles, there is something for everyone in California.

☐ Festivals: Throughout the year, California hosts a variety of cultural festivals that celebrate the state's rich heritage. Some of the most popular include the Coachella Valley Music and Arts Festival, the San Francisco Pride Parade, and the Monterey Jazz Festival.

When visiting California, it is important to be mindful of cultural differences and customs. For example, it is common to tip service workers such as waiters and taxi drivers, and it is considered rude to be loud or disruptive in public spaces. It is also important to be respectful of different cultural beliefs and traditions, and to dress appropriately when visiting religious or cultural sites.

History and Heritage of California

California has a rich and fascinating history that spans back over thousands of years. From the native tribes that inhabited the land, to the arrival of Spanish settlers, and the gold rush of the 1840s, the state has a unique and diverse heritage that has shaped its present-day culture.

California was originally inhabited by a variety of Native American tribes, each with their own language, customs, and way of life. The Spanish arrived in the late 18th century, establishing missions along the coast and setting the stage for the eventual Mexican rule of California.

In 1848, gold was discovered at Sutter's Mill, which sparked the famous California Gold Rush. This event brought thousands of people from all over the world to the state, and quickly transformed California from a remote and sparsely populated territory to a bustling hub of commerce and industry.

As the state continued to grow, California played a pivotal role in several key moments in American history, including the Civil War, World War I and II, and the rise of the Hollywood film industry.

Today, California is home to a diverse and multicultural population, with a rich history that is reflected in its museums, monuments, and cultural celebrations. Visitors can experience the state's heritage by visiting historic sites like San Juan Capistrano Mission, or by taking a tour of Hollywood, where the movie industry was born.

California has a rich history and heritage that spans centuries. from the Spanish to the long-term residents of the area, the indigenous people, colonists who established missions and settlements, California has a unique cultural identity that is still evident today.

California also has a strong connection to the entertainment industry. Hollywood, which is located in Los Angeles, is the center of the film and television industry and is known for producing some of the world's most iconic movies and television shows.

The state is also home to several historic sites, including the historic missions along the California Mission Trail and the Presidio of San Francisco, which was once a military fort and is now a museum and park.

Demographic Diversity

Demographic diversity is one of the defining characteristics of California, a state that is home to a rich mixture of cultures and ethnicities. With a population of over 39 million people, California is the most populous state in the United States, and it is also one of the most diverse. The state's demographic diversity is reflected in its many different cultures, languages, and traditions, all of which contribute to the unique identity of California.

One of the key factors that has contributed to California's demographic diversity is its history of immigration. Throughout the 19th and 20th centuries, millions of people from around the world came to California in search of a better life, including those from China, Mexico, the Philippines, and Europe. Today, California is home to a wide range of ethnic communities, including large populations of Hispanics, Asians, and African Americans.

In addition to its diverse ethnic communities, California is also home to a rich mixture of cultures, religions, and traditions. The state is particularly well known for its thriving arts and culture scene, which is reflected in its many museums, galleries, and theaters. From the vibrant street art of Los Angeles to the iconic Golden Gate Bridge in San Francisco, California is a state that is rich in cultural heritage.

Despite its diversity, California is also a state that is characterized by a strong sense of unity. People from all walks of life come together to celebrate the state's unique culture and heritage, and the state is renowned for its welcoming and inclusive atmosphere. Whether you are a resident or a visitor, California is a state that is sure to leave a lasting impression.

California is known for its diverse population and demographic mix. The state is home to a wide range of ethnic and cultural groups, including Latinx, Asian, African American, and Native American communities. These communities bring their own unique cultural traditions and customs, which can be seen in the state's festivals, food, art, music, and more.

In addition to its diverse demographic makeup, California is also known for its progressive attitude and vibrant LGBTQ+ community. The state has a long history of supporting LGBTQ+ rights, and today it remains one of the most LGBTQ-friendly states in the country.

It is important to note that while California is a place of great diversity, it is also a place where social and economic inequalities exist. Visitors should be aware of the state's complex history and current issues, and respect the communities and cultures they encounter while exploring.

Art and Entertainment:

California is well known for its thriving arts and entertainment scene, reflecting the state's diverse cultural heritage and offering a wide range of options for locals and visitors alike. From world-class museums and performing arts centers to street art and music festivals, the state has something to offer for everyone.

Museums and Art Galleries:

California boasts some of the most prestigious museums and art galleries in the world, including the San Francisco Museum of Modern Art (SFMOMA), the Museum of Contemporary Art in Los Angeles (MOCA), and the Getty Center in Los Angeles. These institutions showcase a variety of art forms, including painting, sculpture, photography, and multimedia, and often host exhibitions by contemporary artists.

Performing Arts:
California is home to numerous performing arts venues, including the renowned Hollywood Bowl and the Dorothy Chandler Pavilion in Los Angeles, and the San Francisco Opera and Ballet. From classical music concerts to jazz and blues performances, the state offers a rich and diverse entertainment scene for music lovers.

Street Art and Murals:
California is also known for its vibrant street art scene, with many cities such as Los Angeles, San Francisco, and Oakland hosting colorful murals and street art installations by local and international artists. These works of art add character and personality to the urban landscape and are a popular tourist attraction.

Music Festivals:

California is a hub for music festivals, with events such as Coachella, Outside Lands, and Stagecoach taking place annually. These festivals attract visitors from all over the world and offer a unique blend of music, art, food, and culture.

California is a hub for art and entertainment, with a vibrant cultural scene that includes world-renowned museums, theaters, music venues, and festivals.

The Los Angeles area is home to a number of museums, including the Getty Center, the Museum of Contemporary Art, and the Los Angeles County Museum of Art (LACMA). San Francisco is also a cultural hub, with institutions like theSan Francisco Museum of Modern Art (SFMOMA), the Contemporary Jewish Museum, and the de Young Museum.

For live entertainment, there are many options to choose from, including Broadway-style shows, concerts, and theater productions. Some of the most famous venues include the Hollywood Bowl, the Greek Theatre, and the Fox Theater. There are also many popular music festivals in the state, such as Coachella, Stagecoach, and Outside Lands.

The entertainment industry is also a major part of California's economy, and the state is home to the headquarters of many major film and television studios. The famous Hollywood Walk of Fame, which honors celebrities from the entertainment industry, is a popular tourist destination.

In conclusion California's rich arts and entertainment scene is a testament to the state's creativity and diversity, and is sure to leave a lasting impression on visitors. From world-class museums and performing arts venues to street art and music festivals, California has something to offer for everyone.

Food and Drinks in California:

California is known for its diverse cuisine that reflects the state's cultural and demographic diversity. With a strong focus on healthy eating and sustainability, Californian cuisine features fresh, seasonal ingredients and a variety of cooking styles, from traditional Mexican to innovative fusion dishes.

One of the most famous foodie destinations in California is the Bay Area, home to renowned restaurants such as Chez Panisse and The French Laundry. San Francisco is also famous for its sourdough bread and seafood, including Dungeness crab and oysters.

Los Angeles is another foodie paradise, known for its diverse street food and diverse ethnic neighborhoods, such as Koreatown, Thai Town, and Little Ethiopia. Some must-try dishes in LA include Korean BBQ, tacos, and pho.

Wine is an integral part of Californian culture, with Napa and Sonoma being two of the world's most famous wine regions. The state produces a wide range of wines, from Cabernet Sauvignon and Chardonnay to Zinfandel and Pinot Noir. Wine tasting and vineyard tours are popular activities for visitors.

California is also known for its innovative craft beer scene, with many local microbreweries and taprooms throughout the state. In San Diego, for example, you can find a thriving beer culture, with a large number of craft breweries producing a wide range of beer styles.

Whether you're a foodie, a wine connoisseur, or just someone who loves to try new and exciting flavors, California has something to offer everyone when it comes to food and drink.

California is a foodie's paradise, with an incredibly diverse array of cuisine. From classic American fare to international cuisine, the state has something for everyone. Some of the most popular dishes in California include Mexican food, seafood, and farm-to-table cuisine.

Mexican food is especially popular in California, due to the state's large Hispanic population. Tacos, burritos, and enchiladas are just a few of the many delicious Mexican dishes that can be found in California. Mexican cuisine is often prepared with fresh, local ingredients, making it healthy and delicious.

Seafood is also a staple in California, with many restaurants serving fresh fish and shellfish caught daily. Some of the most popular seafood dishes in California include clam chowder, crab cakes, and ceviche.

Farm-to-table cuisine is also popular in California, with many restaurants sourcing their ingredients directly from local farms and markets. This type of cuisine emphasizes fresh, seasonal ingredients, and often includes dishes such as salad, grilled meats, and artisanal cheeses.

In addition to its amazing food, California is also known for its thriving wine industry. The state is home to hundreds of wineries, many of which offer tastings and tours. Wine lovers will love exploring the vineyards and tasting rooms of California's wine country, which includes regions such as Napa Valley and Sonoma County.

Mexican Food

Mexican cuisine is one of the most popular and widely available in California, due to the state's close proximity to Mexico and its large Mexican-American population. Some of the staple dishes you can find in California include tacos, burritos, enchiladas, and tamales. Mexican cuisine in California is known for its bold and spicy flavors, as well as its use of fresh ingredients such as avocado, lime, and cilantro.

One of the must-try dishes in California is the carne asada, which is a marinated and grilled flank steak that is often served with warm tortillas, salsa, and guacamole. Another popular dish is the California burrito, which typically includes a flour tortilla filled with seasoned rice, beans, cheese, guacamole, and carne asada or grilled chicken.

For a more authentic Mexican dining experience, visitors can visit Mexican taquerias and cantinas, which are often small, family-owned establishments that serve up traditional Mexican dishes in a lively and colorful atmosphere. Mexican street food is also a popular option in California, with food trucks and street vendors offering a variety of tacos, tortas, and tamales to customers on the go.

Mexican food is widely available throughout California, and you can find it at many restaurants and cafes, including:

- ☐ El Adobe de Capistrano, San Juan Capistrano
- ☐ Guisados, Los Angeles
- ☐ La Taqueria, San Francisco
- ☐ Lolita's Mexican Food, Los Angeles
- ☐ Mercado, Santa Ana
- ☐ Nopalito, San Francisco
- ☐ Taqueria El Farolito, San Francisco
- ☐ Taqueria Los Coyotes, Chula Vista
- ☐ Taqueria Los Pericos, San Diego
- ☐ Taqueria Los Primos, San Jose.

These are just a few of the many options available, and many more Mexican restaurants can be found throughout the state, from the bustling cities to the smaller towns and rural areas. Whether you're in the mood for traditional tacos, hearty burritos, or delicious enchiladas, California has a wealth of Mexican dining options to choose from.

See Food:

Seafood is a staple in California cuisine, with an abundance of fresh seafood available from the Pacific Ocean. Some of the most popular seafood dishes in California include clam chowder, crab cakes, ceviche, fish tacos, and sushi.

Some must-visit seafood restaurants in California include Fisherman's Wharf in San Francisco, which offers fresh seafood dishes like crab and lobster rolls, clam chowder in a bread bowl, and fresh oysters. Monterey Bay Aquarium's Cannery Row in Monterey is another popular spot for seafood, where visitors can enjoy fresh, sustainably sourced seafood dishes while taking in views of the Pacific Ocean. In San Diego, the Coronado area is known for its seafoodrestaurants, with options ranging from casual fish tacos to upscale seafood fine dining.

Additionally, many California farmers' markets and street vendors offer seafood dishes, providing a unique opportunity for visitors to sample the state's diverse seafood offerings while supporting local businesses.

There are several seafood restaurants in California that serve delicious and fresh seafood dishes. Some popular options include:

Fisherman's Wharf, San Francisco: This historic seafood district is famous for its seafood restaurants, seafood stalls and seafood-related attractions.

Monterey's Fisherman's Wharf, Monterey: This popular seafood destination is located nearCannery Row and offers a wide variety of seafood restaurants, seafood markets and seafood-related attractions.

The Crab Station, San Francisco: This seafood restaurant specializes in crab dishes and is popular among locals and tourists alike.

The Crab House, San Francisco: This seafood restaurant is known for its fresh and delicious crab dishes and is a popular place to grab a bite.

The Lobster, Santa Monica: This seafood restaurant is known for its lobster dishes and is a popular spot for locals and tourists alike.

The Hook & Plow, Hermosa Beach: This seafood restaurant is known for its fresh and delicious seafood dishes, and is a popular place to grab a bite.

The Oyster House, San Francisco: This seafood restaurant specializes in oyster dishes and is a popular spot for locals and tourists alike.

Old Fisherman's Grotto in Monterey: This family-owned seafood restaurant has been serving up fresh seafood for over 70 years.

Fish Market in San Mateo: This seafood restaurant is known for its daily fresh fish, oyster bar, and chowder.

The Crab House in San Francisco: This seafood restaurant is famous for its Dungeness crab, lobster, and shrimp.

Here are some of the well-known and popular eateries in California:

1. In-N-Out Burger - Known for its burgers and fries, In-N-Out is a California-based fast food chain.

2. Fisherman's Wharf - Located in San Francisco, Fisherman's Wharf is a seafood market and restaurant where you can find fresh seafood dishes.

3. Slanted Door - A popular restaurant in San Francisco's Ferry Building, Slanted Door offers contemporary Vietnamese cuisine.

4. Spago - A Hollywood-based restaurant that offers California cuisine, Spago is owned by chef Wolfgang Puck.

5.   Chez Panisse - A farm-to-table restaurant in Berkeley, Chez Panisse is known for its seasonal and locally-sourced ingredients.

6. The French Laundry - A three Michelin-starred restaurant in Yountville, The French Laundry is one of the most famous and prestigious restaurants in theworld.

7. Bottega Louie - A gourmet market and restaurant located in Los Angeles, Bottega Louie offers Italian-inspired cuisine and desserts.

8. La Taqueria - A Mexican-style taqueria in San Francisco's Mission District, La Taqueria is famous for its carnitas tacos.

9. Philippe The Original - A historic deli and restaurant in Los Angeles, Philippe

The Original is known for its French dips and pastrami sandwiches.

10. Roscoe's House of Chicken and Waffles - This iconic LA eatery is known for its Southern-style comfort food, including its famous chicken and waffles.

11. Jinya Ramen Bar - With locations throughout Southern California, Jinya Ramen Bar serves up authentic Japanese-style ramen and other dishes in a modern setting.

12. Guerilla Tacos - This LA-based taco truck serves up creative and delicious tacos, made with seasonal and locally-sourced ingredients.

13. The Cheesecake Factory - With locations throughout California, this chain restaurant offers a vast menu of American classics and signature cheesecakes.

14. Gjusta - This Venice-based bakery and deli serves up artisanal breads, cured meats, and other specialties, made with locally-sourced ingredients.

These eateries offer a range of cuisines and dining experiences, from traditional Californian to contemporary fusion. Each offers unique menu items, showcasing the local ingredients and flavors of the state. Whether you're looking for an intimate dinner for two or a larger celebration, California has something to offer for every taste and budget.

Budgeting your Trip to California

Budgeting for a trip to California can be a challenge, but with some planning and research, it's possible to find affordable options without sacrificing quality. Here are some tips to help you budget your trip:

1. Accommodation: Consider staying in budget-friendly options like hostels, budget hotels, and Airbnb rentals instead of more expensive hotels. Look for deals and discounts online, and book in advance to secure the best rates.

2. Transportation: Renting a car is often a convenient option for getting around California, but it can also be expensive. Take into account alternate solutions

like public transportation, car sharing, or ride-hailing services to save money.

3. Food: Eating out can quickly add up, so consider cooking your own meals or eating at food trucks and street vendors to save money. You can also check out grocery stores and farmers markets to purchase fresh and local ingredients.

4. Activities: Many popular attractions in California have a fee, but there are also plenty of free things to do, such as visiting parks, hiking trails, and beaches. Consider purchasing a tourist discount pass, which offers savings on multiple attractions.

5. Shopping: California is known for its high-end shopping, but there are also plenty of budget-friendly options available, such as thrift stores and outlet malls.

6. Planning ahead: Plan your trip in advance to take advantage of early bird

discounts and to secure reservations for popular activities and attractions.

7. Consider alternative accommodations: Instead of staying in a hotel, consider staying in a hostel, Airbnb, or vacation rental. These options can often be much more affordable and offer more space and amenities.

8. Look for free activities: California has a wide range of free activities, such as hiking in the state parks, visiting the beaches, or exploring local street fairs and farmers markets.

9. Bring your own food: Eating out can quickly add up, especially in California where food prices can be high. Consider bringing your own food, such as snacks and drinks, or cooking your own meals.

10. Use coupons and discounts: Look for coupons and discounts for the attractions you want to visit, as well as

for restaurants and shops. You can find these in travel guides, online, or by asking the locals.

11. Be mindful of your spending: Set a budget for your trip and stick to it. Be mindful of your spending and make sure to keep track of your expenses so you don't overspend.

12. Travel during the off-season: California is a popular tourist destination, and prices can be higher during peak season. Consider traveling during the off-season when prices are lower, and crowds are smaller.

13. Travel during the off-season: California is a popular tourist destination, and prices can be higher during peak season. Consider traveling during the off-season when prices are lower, and crowds are smaller.

The average cost of lodging:

The average cost of lodging in California can vary significantly based on a number of factors. including location, time of year, type of accommodation, and level of luxury.

In the popular tourist destinations like San Francisco, Los Angeles, and San Diego, hotels and resorts can range anywhere from $100 to $500 per night for standard rooms. For budget-friendly options, motels and hostels are available for around $50 to $100 per night.

If you are looking for more upscale and luxury accommodations, you can expect to pay anywhere from $500 to $1,000 or more per night for a room in a 5-star hotel or resort.

It's also worth noting that during peak tourist season, prices for all types of accommodations can be significantly higher. On the other hand, if you travel during the off-season, you may be able to find more affordable rates.

Additionally, vacation rental options such as apartments, villas, or condos are also available, which can be a more cost-effective option if you are traveling with a group or family. These can range from $100 to $500 per night, depending on the size, location, and amenities offered.

Accommodation costs in California can vary greatly depending on the location and type of lodging you choose. On average, you can expect to spend anywhere from $80 to $400 per night for a hotel room. However, you may be able to find more budget-friendly options by staying in less touristy areas, opting for budget hotels or hostels, or traveling during the off-season when prices are lower.

It is always a good idea to compare prices from different hotels and online booking websites, and to book in advance to get the best deals. Many hotels also offer discounts for booking directly through their website, so be sure to check for these promotions as well.

Additionally, consider alternative forms of accommodation such as vacation rentals, which can offer more space, privacy, and amenities at a lower cost. Vacation rentals can range from apartments, condos, and houses, and are a great option for families, groups, or those looking for a more home-like experience while on vacation.

Food and drinks Expenses:

Food and drinks expenses can vary widely in California, depending on where you choose to eat and drink. Eating out at a sit-down restaurant can cost anywhere from $15 to $50 or more per person, depending on the type of cuisine and location. Fast food options and street vendors tend to be less expensive, with prices ranging from $5 to $15.

If you're looking to save money on food, consider eating at local grocery stores, where you can purchase fresh produce and ingredients to prepare your own meals. This option can be especially budget-friendly if you're traveling with a group or family.

When it comes to drinks, the cost of a cup of coffee or a beer can range from $3 to $7, depending on the location. Wine is also widely available and can be enjoyed at many restaurants and bars, with prices ranging from $10 to $50 or more for a bottle. If you're interested in trying local wines, consider visiting a winery in California's renowned wine country, where tastings are often offered for a fee.

Food and drinks are a significant part of your budget when traveling in California, with a wide range of options available, from street food and casual cafes to fine-dining restaurants. The average cost of a meal in California varies depending on the location and type of establishment, but it generally ranges from $10 to $30 per person for a main course.

Fast food options are the most affordable, with a combo meal costing around $7 to $10. Sit-down restaurants, on the other hand, can range from $15 to $30 per main course. Seafood, Mexican, and Californian cuisine are popular options, but you'll also find a variety of international cuisine in the state's big cities.

If you're traveling on a budget, there are plenty of affordable options for food and drinks in California, including food trucks, street vendors, and delis. Supermarkets and grocery stores are also an excellent place to stock up on snacks and drinks, and you can save money by cooking your own meals in your accommodation.

You can also enjoy California's famous wine country by taking a tour of the vineyards and wineries, or by trying some of the local wines at a restaurant or bar. A glass of wine in a restaurant typically costs $8 to $15, while a bottle can range from $30 to $100 or more, depending on the type of wine and the location.

It's important to remember that tipping is customary in California, with a recommended amount of 15 to 20% of the total bill in restaurants and bars. When budgeting for your trip, it's a good idea to factor in the cost of tipping to ensure you have enough money for your food and drinks expenses.

Miscellaneous Expenses:

When planning a trip to California, it's important to budget for miscellaneous expenses, which can include things like transportation, entertainment, and souvenirs. Here are a few tips to help you plan for these costs:

- Entertainment: California is home to many world-class attractions, including amusement parks, museums, and theaters. To save money, consider purchasing discount tickets in advance or opting for budget-friendly activities like hiking or visiting local beaches.
- Souvenirs: California is famous for its many unique and high-quality products, including wine, clothing, and artisanal foods. If you're looking to bring home a special keepsake, be prepared to spend a little extra money. To save money, consider purchasing souvenirs at local markets or shopping for items on clearance.

- Use Public Transportation: Instead of using taxis or renting a car, opt for public transportation such as buses or trains to save money on transportation costs.
- Plan ahead: Do research on different accommodation, transportation, and activity options to find the best deals. Make reservations in advance to take advantage of early bird discounts and avoid last-minute price hikes.
- Shop at local markets: Fresh produce and unique items can be purchased at local farmers markets and street vendors. Not only will you be able to try authentic, delicious food, but you'll also be able to save money on expensive meals.
- Take advantage of free activities: Many museums and cultural institutions in California offer free admission on

certain days or for certain groups, so research your options ahead of time.

- Use travel apps and websites: There are many websites and apps that can help you find the best deals on flights, hotels, and activities. Take advantage of these tools to save money and make the most of your trip.
- Be mindful of tips: In California, it's customary to tip service workers, including waiters, bartenders, and hotel staff. Make sure to factor this into your budget when planning your expenses.
- Limit your souvenir purchases: While souvenirs can be fun to bring home, they can also add up quickly. Consider limiting your purchases or opting for cheaper options like postcards or keychains instead of expensive items like t-shirts or mugs.

Money Saving Tips

1. Book your flights, accommodation, and transportation in advance to get the best prices.
2. Consider staying in a budget-friendly accommodation option such as a hostel, Airbnb, or vacation rental.
3. Cook some of your own meals instead of eating out for every meal.
4. Use public transportation instead of taking taxis or renting a car.
5. Take advantage of the many free activities and events available in California, such as hiking, visiting museums, and attending festivals.
6. Shop at local markets and street vendors for souvenirs instead of high-end boutiques.
7. Use discount websites, such as Groupon, to find deals on activities and experiences.

8. Consider visiting off-season to save on travel costs and enjoy fewer crowds.
9. Research and take advantage of any discounts available to students, military personnel, or seniors.

Planning your Itinerary:

When planning an itinerary for a trip to California, there are many factors to consider. First, think about the amount of time you have to spend in the state, as well as your budget, interests, and preferred mode of transportation. Some popular destinations in California include San Francisco, Los Angeles, and San Diego, so it is important to prioritize the places you would like to visit and the activities you would like to do.

If you have a limited amount of time, it may be best to focus on a single city or region, rather than trying to see everything the state has to offer. For example, you might choose to explore San Francisco for a few days, taking in the city's iconic sights, such as the Golden Gate Bridge, Fisherman's Wharf, and Alcatraz Island.

If you have a bit more time, you could expand your itinerary to include other destinations in the Bay Area, such as wine country in Napa and Sonoma, or the scenic coastline along the Pacific Coast Highway. Alternatively, you could travel to Los Angeles to experience the city's beaches, shopping, and entertainment, or head to San Diego to enjoy its year-round warm weather, vibrant cultural scene, and natural beauty.

When planning your itinerary, be sure to also consider practical considerations, such as the time of year you are traveling and the weather conditions in each destination. You may also want to factor in any major events or festivals that may be taking place during your trip, as these can greatly impact your travel experience.

Ultimately, the key to a successful itinerary is to strike a balance between your must-see destinations and your preferred pace of travel. With careful planning, you can create an itinerary that allows you to fully immerse yourself in California's diverse culture, natural beauty, and rich history, while also taking the time to relax and recharge.

California, the Golden State, is a popular travel destination with a wealth of activities and sights to see. Whether you are planning a road trip, a beach holiday, or a city break, there is something for everyone in California. With so much to do, it is important to have a well-planned itinerary to make the most of your time in the state.

Day 1:

- Start in San Francisco and explore Fisherman's Wharf, one of the city's most famous attractions.
- Visit Alcatraz Island and take a guided tour of the former prison.
- Head to Golden Gate Park for a picnic or a stroll among the gardens.
- In the evening, take a walk along the pier at Pier 39 to enjoy the sea lions and a spectacular sunset.

Day 2:

- ☐ Take a scenic drive along the Pacific Coast Highway to Monterey.
- ☐ Stop at the famous 17-Mile Drive to admire the stunning coastline and golf courses.
- ☐ Visit the Monterey Bay Aquarium, one of the largest in the world.

☐ Drive south to Big Sur and hike in the redwoods at Pfeiffer Big Sur State Park.

☐ Stay overnight in the pictures quetown of Carmel-by-the-Sea.

Day 3:

- Continue your drive down the coast to Santa Barbara.
- Spend the day exploring the historic Spanish mission, beaches, and shopping in the town.
- Head to Los Angeles in the evening.

Day 4:

1. Start your day in LA with a visit to the iconic Hollywood Sign.
2. Take a tour of the movie studios and walk down the Hollywood Walk of Fame.

3. Visit the Getty Center for a view of LA and to admire the art collection.
4. End your day with a sunset picnic at Venice Beach.

Day 5:

- Spend the day exploring the theme parks of Anaheim, including Disneyland and California Adventure.
- In the evening, enjoy a baseball game at Angel Stadium or a concert at the Honda Center.

Day 6:

- Head to San Diego for a day of fun in the sun.
- Visit the San Diego Zoo and the USS Midway Museum.

- Spend the afternoon at La Jolla Cove, one of the best snorkeling and scuba diving spots in California.

Day 7:

- Drive back to San Francisco for your final night in California.

Of course, this itinerary is just a suggestion and can be customized to suit your interests and travel style. California is a big state with a lot to see and do, so be sure to give yourself enough time to explore everything you want to see. With a well-planned itinerary and a sense of adventure, you are sure to have a trip of a lifetime in California!

Depending on the kind of experience you're seeking, there isn't a single optimal time to visit California. Every season offers a variety of activities and attractions. Here's a guide to help you choose the best time to visit California based on your interests:

1. Spring (March to May): Spring is a great time to visit California for mild weather and colorful wildflowers. You can enjoy outdoor activities like hiking, cycling, and kayaking, and see the blooming wildflowers in the hills.
2. Summer (June to August): Summer is the peak tourist season in California and is perfect for beach-goers, as the weather is warm and sunny. You can also enjoy outdoor music festivals and cultural events, and visit theme parks like Disneyland and Universal Studios Hollywood.

3. Fall (September to November): Fall is a great time to visit California for cooler weather and fewer crowds. You can enjoy scenic drives, attend wine festivals and tastings, and see the fall foliage in the mountains.

4. Winter (December to February): Winter is a great time to visit California for its mild weather, holiday festivities, and ski season. You can hit the slopes at Lake Tahoe, enjoy the holiday lights in San Francisco, and attend winter festivals in the Napa and Sonoma wine regions.

5. May-June: This is a great time to visit California as the weather is warm, and the wildflowers are in full bloom. This is also a popular time for wine tasting in Napa and Sonoma Valley.

6. November-April: This is the off-season for California tourism and the weather can be cool and rainy, especially in the

northern part of the state. However, this is a great time to visit if you're looking for a quieter and less crowded experience.

It is important to keep in mind that California's weather can be unpredictable, so always be prepared for unexpected changes in the forecast. Regardless of when you visit, there is always something to see and do in California, from its stunning natural landscapes to its rich cultural heritage.

Customizing your Itinerary:

Customizing your itinerary can greatly enhance your experience of California, as it allows you to personalize your trip and prioritize the things that interest you the most. Here are some tips on how to customize your itinerary:

- Consider your interests: Whether you are a nature lover, foodie, or history buff, it's important to choose destinations and activities that align with your interests.
- Research: Research the destinations you're interested in visiting and plan accordingly. Look into the best times to visit, the must-see attractions, and the local customs.
- Plan around the weather: California has a Mediterranean climate with hot summers and mild winters. Consider the weather patterns when planning your trip to ensure that you have the best possible experience.
- Budget - Make sure your itinerary is realistic and matches your budget. California can be expensive, so consider your accommodation, transportation, food, and activities costs when planning.

- Make time for rest and relaxation: While it's important to make the most of your time in California, it's also important to allow time for rest and relaxation. This will help you avoid burnout and ensure that you have a memorable trip.
- Consider a guided tour: If you're visiting California for the first time, you might consider a guided tour. This can help you make the most of your trip, as you'll have a knowledgeable guide to lead you through the state's most popular destinations.
- Seasonal events and activities - California is home to many events and festivals throughout the year, so make sure to check the calendar before you plan your trip. If you're interested in outdoor activities, consider visiting during the warmer months, while those

looking for more indoor activities can plan their trip for the cooler months.

- Personal interests - If you have specific interests like wine tasting, visiting amusement parks, or surfing, make sure to include those activities in your itinerary. You can also find many museums, art galleries, and theaters that cater to these interests.
- Location - California is a large state with many different regions, each with its own unique attractions. Determine which areas you want to visit and how much time you want to spend there to create a manageable itinerary.
- Flexibility - It's always a good idea to build some flexibility into your itinerary in case you want to extend your stay in one place or change your plans. Consider leaving a day or two open to allow for unexpected experiences and impromptu adventures.

- Time of Year: The time of year you visit California can greatly impact your itinerary. Summer is the peak tourist season and prices for accommodations, food and activities can be high, while fall and spring offer more mild weather and often better prices. Winter can be chilly and some tourist destinations may be closed.
- Group Size: If you are traveling with a group, consider everyone's interests and abilities when creating your itinerary. Make sure to balance group activities with solo activities and downtime.

Tips for Solo Travellers

Traveling solo can be an exciting and fulfilling experience, and California offers many opportunities for solo travelers to explore and discover new things. Here are some tips to help make your solo trip to California as smooth and enjoyable as possible:

1. Plan ahead: Before you leave, research your destination, including the places you want to visit, the weather, and any safety considerations. Make a plan for each day, and make sure you have all the necessary travel documents, including your passport and travel insurance.

2. Make sure you have a way to stay in touch with friends and family while you're traveling. Consider getting a local SIM card or using a messaging app that doesn't require an internet connection.

3. Choose safe accommodations: When booking your accommodations, consider staying in a hotel or hostel that is well-reviewed and in a safe location. Avoid staying in remote or isolated areas, and always lock your doors and windows when you're in your room.

4. Be cautious when using public transportation: In California, you'll find many options for getting around, including buses, trains, and taxis. Always be cautious when using public transportation, especially at night, and

consider using a licensed taxi service instead of hailing a cab off the street.

5. Be aware of your surroundings: When exploring new places, always be aware of your surroundings, and trust your instincts. If you feel uncomfortable or unsafe in a particular area, leave immediately.

6. Stay healthy: Make sure you take care of your health while traveling, especially if you're eating and drinking things that are new to you. Pack a first-aid kit, and consider getting any necessary vaccinations before you leave.

7. Make new friends: Going on a solo trip is a fantastic way to meet new people. Consider joining a tour or taking a class to meet like-minded travelers. You can also join social media groups or use apps to connect with other travelers.

8. Be open-minded: Traveling solo allows you to experience new cultures and customs, and it's important to be open-minded and respectful. Don't judge people based on their culture, religion, or lifestyle, and always ask permission before taking photos of people or places.

9. Plan your itinerary beforehand and let someone know about your plans. This way, someone will know where you are and when you should be back.

10. Be aware of the local customs and culture. Learn the basic phrases in the local language to help you get by.

11. Research your accommodation options and choose wisely. You can opt for a hostel, hotel or Airbnb, but always read the reviews and be aware of the location and safety.

12. Keep your valuables close to you at all times and never leave them unattended.

13. Join a tour group or take a guided tour. This can be a great way to meet other travelers and get to know the area better.

14. Be mindful of your belongings and keep your backpack or purse close to you. Use a money belt or secure your valuables in a locker when you're not using them.

15. Don't be afraid to ask for help. Whether it's from the locals, hotel staff or fellow travelers, don't hesitate to reach out if you need assistance.

Transportation and lodging:

When it comes to choosing accommodation and transportation as a solo traveler, it's important to consider safety, comfort, and budget.

Accommodation:

☐ Research the location thoroughly before booking. Look for accommodations in well-lit and populated areas, especially if you're traveling alone.

☐ Consider staying in hostels, which can be a budget-friendly option and also a great way to meet other travelers.

☐ Choose accommodations with secure lockers and 24/7 reception, especially if you're traveling with valuable items.

☐ Take advantage of online reviews and feedback to get a sense of the quality of the accommodation.

Transportation:

☐ Invest in a good quality backpack and lock to secure your belongings while traveling.

☐ Use public transportation, especially during the day, when it is generally safe and convenient.

☐ Avoid using taxis, especially at night, and opt for ride-sharing services like Uber or Lyft, instead.

☐ Consider purchasing a travel insurance policy to cover unexpected costs and incidents during your trip.

☐ Plan your routes and have backup options in case of unexpected incidents.

☐ Plan ahead: Research your destinations and make sure you have a clear understanding of the local culture, customs, and language. It's always best to be prepared and have a basic understanding of the local norms to avoid any miscommunications or cultural faux pas.

☐ Stay connected: Make sure you have a way to stay connected while you're on the road, either through a local SIM card or a global Wi-Fi device. This will allow you to stay in touch with friends and family, navigate using maps, and access information about your destinations.

☐ Stay safe: When traveling solo, it's important to be aware of your surroundings and take necessary precautions to stay safe. Keep valuables close, trust your instincts, and be mindful of your actions in unfamiliar places.

☐ Take time for self-care: Traveling can be tiring, especially if you're doing it alone. Make sure you take time for self-care and prioritize rest and relaxation to ensure you have an enjoyable and memorable trip.

☐ Choose the right accommodation: Consider your budget and the level of comfort and security you need when selecting your accommodation. Look for hotels with 24-hour front desks, secure locks on doors, and good reviews from other solo travelers. Hostels and vacation rentals can also be a good option for solo travelers who are looking to save money and meet other travelers.

☐ Plan your transportation: Decide whether you prefer public transportation, rental cars, taxis, or ridesharing services, and research the options available in your destination. Consider safety and cost when making your decision. Make sure to familiarize yourself with the local transportation system and take advantage of online resources to find the best deals.

By following these tips, you can have a safe and enjoyable solo trip to California. Whether you're exploring the beaches, hiking in the mountains, or experiencing the city life, you're sure to have a memorable experience.

Glossary:

Glossary: A glossary is a list of words and their definitions that are connected to a certain subject or industry. In the context of travel, a glossary can help familiarize travelers with the language and terminology commonly used in the industry. Here are some important terms for travelers visiting California:

- Accommodation: refers to a place to stay while traveling, such as a hotel, hostel, vacation rental, or campground.
- Itinerary: a plan or route for a trip, including the places you will visit and the activities you will participate in.
- Transportation: refers to the means of getting from one place to another, such as by car, bus, train, or airplane.
- Budget: a plan for spending money on a trip, including estimates for expenses

such as accommodation, food, transportation, and entertainment.

- Tourist attraction: a site or destination that is popular with visitors, such as a theme park, museum, historical site, or natural wonder.
- Guidebook: a book that provides information and advice on travel, including details on destinations, attractions, and activities.
- Solo travel: traveling alone without the company of a travel companion.
- Hostel: a type of accommodation that offers shared dormitory-style rooms at a low cost.
- Vacation rental: a type of accommodation that provides a private space for travelers, such as a house or apartment.
- Campground: an area designated for camping, often with facilities for tents or recreational vehicles.

- Pacific Time Zone: California is in the Pacific Time Zone, which is 3 hours behind Eastern Standard Time.
- California State Parks: There are over 280 state parks in California, which offer a range of activities and attractions, such as hiking, camping, and scenic drives.
- Yosemite National Park: One of the most famous national parks in California, Yosemite is known for its towering granite cliffs, waterfalls, and diverse wildlife.
- Golden Gate Bridge: A famous suspension bridge in San Francisco, the Golden Gate Bridge connects the city to Marin County and is a popular tourist attraction.
- Hollywood: A neighborhood in Los Angeles, Hollywood is famous for its movie industry and attractions such as

the Walk of Fame and the Hollywood Sign.

- Santa Cruz Beach Boardwalk: A seaside amusement park in Santa Cruz, the Santa Cruz Beach Boardwalk is a popular destination for families and visitors of all ages.
- Lake Tahoe: A large freshwater lake located in the Sierra Nevada mountain range, Lake Tahoe is popular for its scenic beauty, water sports, and ski resorts.
- Monterey Bay Aquarium: A public aquarium located in Monterey, the Monterey Bay Aquarium is one of the largest and most diverse aquariums in the world.
- San Diego Zoo: A famous zoo located in San Diego, the San Diego Zoo is known for its wide variety of species and conservation efforts.

Words used in California and Phrases

- "The Valley" - refers to the San Fernando Valley, a large urbanized valley located in Los Angeles
- "The OC" - abbreviation for Orange County
- "SoCal" - abbreviation for Southern California
- "The Bay" - refers to the San Francisco Bay Area
- "Hella" - a slang term used to mean "very" or "a lot"
- Chill" - means to relax or take it easy
- "Bro" - a slang term used to refer to a male friend
- "The City" - refers to San Francisco
- "The Beach" - refers to the coastal areas in California
- "Laid back" - means relaxed and casual
- "Stoked" - means excited or enthusiastic
- Rad" - means cool or awesome.

- "The Inland Empire" - refers to the metropolitan area located in Riverside and San Bernardino counties
- "The Coast" - refers to the California coastline.
- "Surf's up" - a greeting used by surfers to indicate good waves for surfing.
- Dude": This is a casual term used to address someone, often used between friends.
- Foggy": This term is used to describe the thick and persistent coastal fog that can occur in certain areas of California.
- "Cali": A nickname for California.

Key People and Places

California is known for its vibrant culture, diverse communities, and rich history. It is home to many famous people and iconic places that have made a significant impact on the state and the world. Here are some of the key people and places in California:

- Hollywood: Hollywood is a neighborhood in Los Angeles, California that is famous for its film industry. The Hollywood Sign, a 14-meter tall white letter that spells "HOLLYWOOD" on the hills, is one of the most famous landmarks in the world.
- San Francisco: San Francisco is a city that is famous for its iconic Golden Gate Bridge, Fisherman's Wharf, and Alcatraz Island. The city is known for its Victorian architecture, diverse communities, and scenic beauty.

- Silicon Valley: Silicon Valley is a region in northern California that is home to many of the world's largest technology companies, including Google, Apple, and Facebook. The area is known for its high-tech innovation and entrepreneurial spirit.
- Steve Jobs: Steve Jobs was an American entrepreneur and inventor who co-founded Apple Inc. He was a pioneer in the personal computer revolution and helped to bring the graphical user interface to personal computers.
- Mark Zuckerberg: Mark Zuckerberg is an American technology entrepreneur and the co-founder of Facebook. He is one of the youngest billionaires in the world and is known for his philanthropic work.
- Oprah Winfrey: Oprah Winfrey is an American media executive, actress, and

philanthropist. She is best known for her talk show, "The Oprah Winfrey Show," which was the highest-rated television program of its kind in history.

- The California Museum: The California Museum is a history museum located in Sacramento, California. It is dedicated to telling the story of California and its people through interactive exhibits and educational programs.

- Monterey Bay Aquarium: The Monterey Bay Aquarium is a public aquarium located in Monterey, California. It is one of the largest aquariums in the world and is known for its exhibitions of marine life from the Pacific Ocean.

- Yosemite National Park: Yosemite National Park is a national park located in the Sierra Nevada Mountains of

California. It is known for its breathtaking scenery, including waterfalls, valleys, meadows, and granite cliffs.

- Alcatraz Island: Alcatraz Island is a small island located in San Francisco Bay. It was once a federal prison and is now a popular tourist destination. Visitors can tour the prison and learn about its history and the famous inmates who were incarcerated there.

These are just a few of the key people and places in California that travelers should be aware of. By exploring these iconic locations and learning about their history and significance, travelers can gain a deeper appreciation for the state and its rich heritage.

Places in California

California is one of the largest states in the United States, so there are many great places to explore! The following are a some of the most well-liked locations:

- San Francisco - Known for its iconic Golden Gate Bridge, bustling Fisherman's Wharf, and the hilly streets of the city's famous neighborhoods, San Francisco is a must-visit city in California.
- Los Angeles - From its famous beaches, like Venice and Santa Monica, to its iconic Hollywood sign, there's no shortage of things to see and do in Los Angeles. It's also home to a number of famous museums, including the Getty Center and the Museum of Contemporary Art.
- San Diego - With its sunny beaches, world-class museums, and vibrant

cultural scene, San Diego is a popular destination for both tourists and locals.

- Yosemite National Park - Located in the Sierra Nevada Mountains, Yosemite National Park is one of California's most beautiful natural wonders. With its towering peaks, sparkling waterfalls, and diverse wildlife, it's an ideal destination for outdoor enthusiasts.
- Lake Tahoe - This stunning alpine lake is surrounded by mountains and forests, and is a popular destination for skiing, snowboarding, and water sports.
- Monterey Bay - With its beautiful beaches, scenic coastline, and rich marine life, Monterey Bay is a must-visit destination for anyone traveling to California.

These are only a few of the amazing locations in California. Whether you're looking for adventure, relaxation, or cultural experiences, there's something for everyone in this diverse and beautiful state.

Transportation Terminology

Transportation terminology can be confusing for travelers, especially when visiting a new place. California, being a large state, has a variety of modes of transportation and it's important to understand the lingo to make getting around easier. Here are some common transportation terms used in California:

1. Bus: A mode of public transportation that travels on a fixed route and stops at designated locations along the way.
2. Train: A mode of transportation that operates on tracks and runs between stations. In California, trains are operated by Amtrak, Caltrain, and Metrolink.
3. Light Rail: A type of train that operates on a fixed route, typically in urban

areas, and is powered by overhead electrical wires.

4. Cable Car: A type of transportation that uses a cable and runs on a fixed route, often in hilly areas. San Francisco is famous for its cable cars, which are considered a National Historic Landmark.

5. Streetcar: A type of transportation that operates on tracks and runs along streets, usually in urban areas.

6. Ferry: A mode of transportation that carries passengers and vehicles across a body of water. In California, ferries are often used to travel between San Francisco and the nearby islands.

7.

8. Subway: A mode of transportation that operates on tracks and travels underground in a city.

9. BART: The Bay Area Rapid Transit is a heavy rail public transportation

system that serves the San Francisco Bay Area.

10. Trolley: A type of train that operates on tracks and is powered by overhead electrical wires.

11. Ride Sharing: A service where individuals can request a ride through a smartphone app, and be picked up and dropped off by a private driver. Uber and Lyft are popular ride-sharing companies in California.

12. Freeway: A type of road in California with high-speed, limited-access, divided traffic lanes.

13. High-Occupancy Vehicle (HOV) Lane: A type of road lane in California that is restricted to vehicles with more than one occupant, such as carpools or vanpools.

Appendix

An appendix is a section at the end of a document that includes supplementary information. It is not essential to the main content but provides additional information that might be helpful or of interest to the reader. The purpose of an appendix is to provide context or support for the information presented in the main body of the document.

In a travel guide for California, an appendix might include information such as:

1. List of Public Holidays: A list of public holidays in California, along with the dates and significance, can be added to the appendix to help travelers plan their trip accordingly.

2. Emergency Information: Information such as emergency phone numbers, medical facilities, and consulates can

be included in the appendix to help travelers in case of an emergency.

3. Money Matters: Information on currency exchange rates, ATMs, and banks in California can be added to the appendix to help travelers plan their finances.

4. Local Festivals & Events: A list of festivals and events that take place in California, along with their dates, can be added to the appendix to help travelers plan their trip around them.

5. Weather: A table or chart that provides average temperatures and weather patterns for different regions in California can be added to the appendix to help travelers plan their outfits and activities.

6. Packing List: A comprehensive packing list that includes items to bring for different types of activities and

weather conditions can be added to the appendix to help travelers prepare for their trip.

7. Currency conversion rates - The appendix can include up-to-date currency conversion rates to help travelers budget their expenses.

8. Health and safety tips - Information on health and safety in the area can help travelers prepare for any potential risks and take necessary precautions.

Important phone Numbers and Websites:

When traveling to California, it's important to have access to important phone numbers and websites in case of any emergency or for getting information on various aspects of the trip. Some of the important phone numbers and websites are:

- Emergency services - 911

- California Highway Patrol - (800) 835-5247
- Tourist information centers - Visit California (www.visitcalifornia.com)
- Los Angeles International Airport (LAX) - (855) 463-5252
- San Diego International Airport (SAN) - (619) 400-2404
- Public transportation information - 511 (www.511.org)
- California Amtrak - (800) 872-7245
- California Department of Transportation (Caltrans) - (916) 654-5266
- California National Parks Service - (209) 372-0259

It's a good idea to also research and add information on local transportation services, rental car companies, and taxi or ride-share services in the area you will be visiting. Furthermore, it's wise to constantly carry a hard copy of these phone numbers and websites as a backup, in case of any issues with internet connectivity.

Climate and Weather Data:

Climate and weather play a significant role in determining the travel plans of visitors to California. The state has a diverse range of climates and weather patterns, with the coastal regions being relatively temperate and the inland regions being hotter and drier.

The coastal regions of California, such as San Francisco and Los Angeles, typically experience cool and foggy conditions, with temperatures ranging from 50 to 60 degrees Fahrenheit. The inland regions, such as Sacramento and San Bernardino, have hot and dry summers with temperatures reaching over 100 degrees Fahrenheit. Winter in California is mild, with occasional rain and snow in the mountains.

Visitors to California should be prepared for the weather and pack accordingly. For coastal regions, a light jacket or sweater is recommended, while for the inland regions, light and breathable clothing is recommended. Sunscreen and a hat are also important items to bring, especially during the summer months.

Climate and weather data can be obtained from various sources such as the National Weather Service, local news stations, and travel websites. It is always important to check the weather forecast before your trip to California to make sure you are prepared for the conditions you will encounter.

The climate and weather of California varies greatly depending on the region and the time of year. Coastal areas generally have a Mediterranean climate with mild, wet winters and warm, dry summers. Inland areas, such as the Central Valley, experience hot summers and cool winters with occasional frosts.

The average temperature in the coastal regions of California is around 60-70°F (15-21°C), while temperatures in the inland areas can reach up to 90-100°F (32-38°C). During the summer, temperatures in the desert regions can soar to well over 100°F (38°C).

If you're traveling to California during the winter, it's a good idea to pack a light jacket or sweater, as temperatures can drop significantly in the evenings. In the summer, pack lightweight clothing and a hat to protect yourself from the sun.

Travel Apps and Technology:

Travel apps and technology have revolutionized the way we travel, making the experience smoother, easier, and more convenient. Some of the most useful travel apps and technology for travelers visiting California include:

- Travel booking apps: Apps like Expedia, Booking.com, and Airbnb make it easy to find and book your accommodations, flights, and activities.
- Transportation apps: Uber and Lyft are two popular ride-hailing services that are widely available in California. There are also many transportation apps specific to the state, such as CalTrain and Bay Area Rapid Transit (BART), that provide schedules and real-time updates for local trains and buses.
- Language translation apps: Google Translate and iTranslate are popular language translation apps that can help

you navigate California and communicate with locals, even if you don't speak the same language.

- Weather apps: Accuweather and Weather Underground are two popular weather apps that provide real-time weather updates and forecasts, making it easier to plan your activities and avoid inclement weather.
- Google Maps - a must-have app for navigation and finding directions. You can use it offline as well, making it a great tool for exploring California without incurring data charges.
- Yelp - a local review and recommendation app that can help you find the best restaurants, cafes, and shops in California. You can read reviews and see photos of each location, making it easy to decide where to go.
- Uber or Lyft - these ride-sharing apps are a convenient and affordable way to get around California. Simply download the app, enter your pickup and drop-off You'll

be matched with a driver in a matter of minutes and locations.

- Hopper - this app is perfect for travelers who want to save money on flights. Hopper predicts future prices and tells you when is the best time to buy your plane ticket.
- Wifi Map - a useful app that helps you find free Wi-Fi hotspots in California. This app can save you money on data charges and ensure you always have an internet connection when you need it.

Conclusion

The conclusion is an important section of your travel guide as it provides a summary of the key points and insights you've shared throughout the guide. When writing the conclusion of your guide to California, here are some key points to consider:

- Recap of the main attractions: Briefly summarize the main attractions and places of interest that you've discussed in your guide.
- Key takeaways: Highlight the most important tips and advice you've shared in your guide, such as budgeting tips, transportation options, and safety considerations.
- Reflection on California as a destination: Share your thoughts and impressions about California as a travel destination. Was it what you expected? Would you recommend it to others?
- Final thoughts: Offer some final words of encouragement and advice to travelers who are planning a trip to California. Encourage them to explore, be open-minded, and make the most of their time in this beautiful state.
- Call to action: End your conclusion with a call to action, encouraging

readers to share their own experiences and feedback, or to contact you with questions or comments.

Traveling to California can be a wonderful and exciting experience for any traveler, whether solo or in a group. With its diverse and rich culture, stunning natural beauty, and endless entertainment options, California has something to offer for everyone. However, it is important to plan ahead, budget well, and be prepared for the various expenses involved in your trip. Additionally, familiarizing yourself with the local customs, language, and transportation options can enhance your travel experience and make it smoother. By following these tips, you can have an unforgettable trip to California and make memories that will last a lifetime.

A trip to California can be a once-in-a-lifetime experience filled with endless possibilities. To ensure a successful trip, it is important to plan ahead and consider your budget, travel itinerary, and safety. Additionally, familiarizing yourself with the language, culture, and climate of the area can greatly enhance your experience.

When it comes to future travel, it is recommended to regularly check for updates on travel restrictions and guidelines, as well as to remain flexible with your plans. In terms of recommendation, consider visiting during the shoulder season (spring or fall) to avoid peak tourist season and take advantage of more manageable crowds and potentially lower prices.

It is also recommended to stay connected and make use of travel apps and technology to make the most out of your trip. Having important phone numbers and websites at hand, as well as being aware of the climate and weather data, can also come in handy in ensuring a smooth and enjoyable journey.

Finally, it is important to keep an open mind and be flexible, as well as to be mindful of the local culture and customs. Remember to enjoy the experience, take in the sights, and make lasting memories.

In the future, California will continue to be a popular travel destination for its diverse landscape, rich cultural heritage, and exciting entertainment offerings. It is highly recommended to visit this beautiful state and explore all it has to offer.

With these tips, you'll be well on your way to a successful and memorable trip to California.

Remember, the key to a successful trip is preparation and a willingness to embrace new experiences. Take time to research and plan ahead, but also be open to the unexpected. Above all, relax, have fun, and enjoy the journey. And who knows, your trip to California might just inspire you to plan your next adventure to another exciting destination.

Printed in Great Britain
by Amazon

19645977R00108